Tomorrow Never Comes

Written by Joanna Nadin
Illustrated by Marion Lindsay

OXFORD
UNIVERSITY PRESS

OXFORD
UNIVERSITY PRESS

Great Clarendon Street, Oxford, OX2 6DP, United Kingdom

Oxford University Press is a department of the University of Oxford. It furthers the University's objective of excellence in research, scholarship, and education by publishing worldwide. Oxford is a registered trade mark of Oxford University Press in the UK and in certain other countries

Text © Joanna Nadin 2017
Illustrations © Marion Lindsay 2017
Inside cover notes written by Karra McFarlane

The moral rights of the author have been asserted

First published 2017

All rights reserved. No part of this publication may be reproduced, stored in a retrieval system, or transmitted, in any form or by any means, without the prior permission in writing of Oxford University Press, or as expressly permitted by law, by licence or under terms agreed with the appropriate reprographics rights organization. Enquiries concerning reproduction outside the scope of the above should be sent to the Rights Department, Oxford University Press, at the address above.

You must not circulate this work in any other form and you must impose this same condition on any acquirer

British Library Cataloguing in Publication Data
Data available

ISBN: 978-0-19-841513-8

10 9 8 7

Paper used in the production of this book is a natural, recyclable product made from wood grown in sustainable forests. The manufacturing process conforms to the environmental regulations of the country of origin.

Printed in China by Shanghai Offset Printing Products Ltd

Acknowledgements

Series Editor: Nikki Gamble

Mabel had nothing to do.

So she went to see Dad.

"Can we go to the circus?" Mabel asked.

"Maybe tomorrow, Mabel," said Dad. "I'm far too busy."

But tomorrow came, and Dad was still busy.

So Mabel went to see Mum.

"Can we go to the zoo?" she asked.

"Maybe tomorrow, Mabel," said Mum. "I'm far too busy."

But tomorrow came, and Mum was still busy.

So Mabel went to see Grandpa.

"Can we go to the beach?" she asked.

"Maybe tomorrow, Mabel," said Grandpa. "I'm far too busy."

"That's what everyone says!" Mabel shouted. "But they're always busy, and tomorrow never comes."

She went up the stairs to her bedroom to sulk.

As she lay on her bed, Mabel made a plan.

"If everyone is far too busy, I will have adventures all by myself," she said.

First, Mabel swung around her room with four naughty monkeys.

They made a terrible mess of the bookshelves.

Next, she had a tea party with seven silly soldiers.

They made a terrible mess of the carpet.

Then she did a dance with twelve dangerous dinosaurs.

They made a terrible mess of the walls.

Finally, she had a game of hide-and-seek with fifteen sneaky sheep.

They made a terrible mess of *everything*!

Grandpa knocked on Mabel's door.

"Do you want to go to the beach?" he asked.

"Maybe tomorrow," said Mabel.
"I'm a bit busy."

And she went back to her adventures.

Mum knocked on Mabel's door.

"Do you want to go to the zoo?" she asked.

"Maybe tomorrow," said Mabel.
"I'm a bit busy."

And she went back to her adventures.

Dad knocked on Mabel's door.

"It's an awful mess in here," he said. "What have you been doing?"

"I've been having adventures," said Mabel.

"Well, I think it's time to tidy up," said Dad.

Mabel smiled.

"Maybe tomorrow," she said. "I'm busy."